INCLUSION FOR THE MIDDLE SCHOOL SOCIAL STUDIES CLASSROOM

STRATEGIES AND ACTIVITIES

Glencoe
McGraw-Hill

New York, New York   Columbus, Ohio   Woodland Hills, California   Peoria, Illinois

Glencoe/McGraw-Hill

*A Division of The **McGraw·Hill** Companies*

Send all inquiries to:
Glencoe/McGraw-Hill
8787 Orion Place
Columbus, OH 43240

ISBN 0-07-823138-8

Printed in the United States of America.

3 4 5 6 7 8 9 10 108 04 03 02

CONTENTS

CHAPTER III—CIVICS

CHAPTER IV—GEOGRAPHY

What Is an Inclusive Classroom?

Education for special needs students (ranging from learning disabled to gifted) has progressed from the isolation environment to the total-inclusive environment. On the evolutionary road to inclusion, students were "mainstreamed" into the general education classroom. Mainstreaming meant that children were in a regular classroom for part of the day to interact with other students and returned to their special classrooms for small group instruction and activities. Administrators, teachers, parents, and students witnessed the success of mainstreaming as students learned in environments that included students with various learning abilities. Mainstreaming also allowed the students to develop socially and emotionally as they interacted with all types of students.

In the 1990s, special needs students were assigned to general education classrooms for all subjects. Classroom teachers and specialists worked closely together to develop individual educational programs for these students in the classroom. The inclusive classroom is based on the concept that all students can learn from each other despite their learning capabilities. At the end of the twentieth century and extending into the twenty-first century, several new terms were introduced to describe an inclusive classroom, including the mixed-ability classroom or differentiated learning. Another change is the name applied to the learning disabled student—the struggling student.

Teaching in a Mixed-Ability Classroom

Teaching today has different challenges than it did 10 years ago. This is especially true at the middle school level where most social studies teachers have both students preparing for college-prep high school courses and struggling students in the same class. Teachers today are not only expected to have defined *outcomes* for their courses, but they are also expected to help all of these students achieve these outcomes despite the wide-range of students' interests, talents, or abilities.

Because of the demands of mixed-ability classrooms, teachers sometimes need help with effectively connecting the subject to the needs and abilities of their students. This book hopes to provide teachers with strategies that will support *all learners*—from highly capable learners to struggling learners. By using these strategies—or adaptations of them—on a routine basis, teachers will more easily create differentiated classrooms where instruction, learning tasks, and assessment approaches are adjusted according to the students' needs and abilities. Teachers can use these strategies as they are presented and then explore ways to design their own activities that will help students organize, remember, and think more critically about social studies.

Teaching Strategies for the Social Studies Inclusive Classroom

While this book provides teachers with resources to help support struggling learners, most of these strategies will be effective with all learners. A brief description of these strategies follows.

- **Instructional Adaptations**—Teachers are provided with several ways of modifying their instruction to meet the varied needs of their students.

- **Organizing and Remembering**—In addition to helpful student tips, graphic organizers are used on student pages to help students break down the material into manageable pieces which are easier to organize and remember.

- **Cooperative Learning Strategies**—Almost all of the activities can be adapted for use in pairs ("thinking partners") or in small groups ("thinking quads"). Students often learn better when they share and clarify their thoughts with peers. It is important that students know their roles in the cooperative learning group (for example, the assigned roles of leader, recorder, reporter, timekeeper, researcher, artist, etc.). This ensures that each student completes his or her share of the work in a group setting.

- **Higher Level Thinking**—Student pages offer open-ended questions to enable students to enrich and expand their learning.

- **Alternative Assessment Strategies**—Every teacher page contains ways to adapt the students' assessments to more closely reflect the various ways that adolescents can demonstrate what they have learned. In addition, some strategies, such as the One-Minute Paper, not only focus the students on what they have learned, but also help the teacher identify areas of confusion.

- **Multidimensional Rubrics**—Before giving an assignment, teachers should prepare a rubric that will guide students in preparing a project, researching a paper, or answering an essay question. In mixed-ability classrooms, teachers are encouraged to use multidimensional rubrics to score open-ended questions. This type of rubric allows for differentiated feedback. With a multidimensional rubric, a teacher can provide a student with separate ratings: one that provides feedback on the content and one that focuses on written/oral communication. Since instruction methods, teaching strategies, and students vary from one class to another, preparation for rubrics are suggested but not displayed in this book.

- **Repetition of Activities**—All students need to feel comfortable with directions and activities in order to succeed. Repetition is particularly helpful for struggling students. For this reason, several activities are repeated for content material throughout the book.

ACTIVITY 1 TEACHING STRATEGY
Finding and Organizing Details

TOPIC: American History—Major European Explorers

STUDENT ACTIVITY: Completing a Matrix

◆ **RATIONALE**

- Students will develop a concrete understanding of the key terms and concepts.

- Students will broaden their understanding about major European explorers.

- By identifying how concepts are similar and how they are different, students will have details about the topic to use when answering open-ended questions.

- Students will use their knowledge to answer higher-level thinking questions.

◆ **OBJECTIVE**

- Students will have a contextual and comparative understanding of the major European explorers (1487–1682).

◆ **ENGAGEMENT**

- Teacher can present a transparency of a completed matrix on a topic, such as famous artists or television characters. Teacher asks questions that require students to use the data on the matrix, such as *Which famous person is from England?*

◆ **INSTRUCTIONAL SUPPORT**

- Make and use a transparency of the worksheet to demonstrate to the class how to complete it.

- Allow students to work with partners to complete the worksheet.

- Partially complete the worksheet for some students.

- While some students are still working, ask students who have finished to answer the "To Think About" questions.

- Ask sets of "thinking partners" to form "thinking quads" to discuss answers.

- After students have completed the worksheet, lead a discussion on the exercise.

- Encourage students to use the worksheet when studying for the test.

◆ **ASSESSMENT SUPPORT**

- During examinations, provide students with a blank or partially completed matrix worksheet to assist them to organize their thoughts before answering test questions, or allow students to use completed matrix worksheets when answering open-ended and higher-level thinking questions.

ACTIVITY 1: Major European Explorers

Finding and Organizing Details

STUDENT TIPS:
- A chart can help you organize information when there are many details.
- Make sure you write the information in the correct box.

DIRECTIONS:
Use your textbook and other resources to complete this chart.

MAJOR EUROPEAN EXPLORERS			
COUNTRY	EXPLORER	DATES	ACHIEVEMENTS
ENGLAND			
FRANCE			
PORTUGAL			
SPAIN			

◆ TO THINK ABOUT:
- Why do you think many people speak Portuguese in Brazil and English in the United States?
- Are there explorers in the twenty-first century? If so, what places are they exploring?

2

ACTIVITY 2 TEACHING STRATEGY
Finding and Organizing Details

• •

TOPIC: American History—History of Massachusetts
STUDENT ACTIVITY: Creating a Newspaper Page

◆ **RATIONALE**

• Students will increase their knowledge of the history of Massachusetts through research and asking questions.

• Students will explore different styles of writing about an event or a person—the feature article or the interview.

◆ **OBJECTIVES**

• Students will be familiar with an important event in the history of Massachusetts.

• Students will use research skills, critical thinking skills, and writing skills.

◆ **ENGAGEMENT**

• Teacher can begin class by discussing a current event described in a newspaper. Teacher should guide students to see how the article addresses the questions *who, what, where, when,* and *why.* The class is divided into teams of three and each team should create a newspaper article related to the event.

◆ **INSTRUCTIONAL SUPPORT**

• Show sample newspapers or make suggestions to the class on various approaches to creating a newspaper using programs such as The Print Shop®, Microsoft Word®, AppleWorks®, or Adobe PageMaker®.

• Allow students to work with partners or small teams to complete the project.

• Supply students with sample interview questions.

• Require students with special needs to use an adapted format.

• Midway through the project, ask students to share their progress and offer suggestions to their classmates.

◆ **ASSESSMENT SUPPORT**

• During examinations, allow students to use their completed pages when answering open-ended and higher-level thinking questions.

ACTIVITY 2: History of Massachusetts

Finding and Organizing Details

STUDENT TIPS:
- To help you find information and pictures for your newspaper, try these Internet search tools:

  Online Britannica: **www.britannica.com**

  The United States Library of Congress: **www.loc.gov/exhibits**
- Look at different newspapers to see how pages are designed.

DIRECTIONS:

Create the front page of a newspaper reporting one of the events listed below. Include a newspaper banner, a headline, a feature story, and an interview with one of the participants.

Your feature story should answer these questions:

- *Who* was involved in the event?
- *What* happened?
- *Where* and *when* did this event take place?
- *Why* was this important at the time?

Your interview should help the reader see, hear, and feel the emotion of the event from a participant's point of view. Summarize the interview as an essay or a question and answer format.

Events

—The Pilgrims' Journey

—The Signing of the Mayflower Compact

—The First Thanksgiving

—King Philip's War

◆ TO THINK ABOUT:
- What would some news topics have been during the Pilgrims' first year in Massachusetts? Who would the readers have been?
- Read a feature columnist's column in your local newspaper. What types of writing techniques did he or she use that are similar to yours?

ACTIVITY 3 TEACHING STRATEGY
Finding and Organizing Details

TOPIC: American History—New England Colonies
STUDENT ACTIVITY: Completing a Matrix

◆ RATIONALE

- Students will develop a concrete under-standing of the key terms and concepts.

- Students will broaden their under-standing about the New England colonies.

- By identifying how concepts are similar and how they are different, students will have details about the topic to use when answering open-ended questions.

- Students will use their knowledge to answer higher-level thinking questions.

◆ OBJECTIVE

- Students will have a contextual and com-parative understanding of the founders of the New England colonies.

◆ ENGAGEMENT

- Teacher can present a transparency of a completed matrix on a topic such as foot-ball franchises or music groups. Teacher asks questions that require students to use the data on the matrix such as *Which franchise was founded first?*

◆ INSTRUCTIONAL SUPPORT

- Make and use a transparency of the worksheet to demonstrate to the class how to complete it.

- Allow students to work with partners to complete the worksheet.

- Partially complete the worksheet for some students.

- While some students are still working, ask students who have finished to answer the "To Think About" questions.

- Ask sets of "thinking partners" to form "thinking quads" to discuss answers.

- After students have completed the work-sheet, lead a discussion on the exercise.

- Encourage students to use the worksheet when studying for the test.

◆ ASSESSMENT SUPPORT

- During examinations, provide students with a blank or partially completed matrix worksheet to assist them in organizing their thoughts before answering test questions, or allow stu-dents to use completed matrix work-sheets when answering open-ended and higher-level thinking questions.

ACTIVITY 3: New England Colonies

Finding and Organizing Details

STUDENT TIPS:
- When you write information in the chart, move across the boxes rather than down so that you do not get the categories confused.
- Make sure you write the correct information in the correct category.

DIRECTIONS:
Use your textbook and other resources to complete this chart.

NEW ENGLAND COLONIES			
COLONY	FOUNDER	DATE FOUNDED	REASON WHY IT WAS FOUNDED
MASSACHUSETTS • **Massachusetts Bay Colony** • **Plymouth**			
NEW HAMPSHIRE			
RHODE ISLAND			
CONNECTICUT			

◆ TO THINK ABOUT:
- Which colonies were founded for religious freedom?
- Are there any groups persecuted today for their beliefs?

ACTIVITY 4 TEACHING STRATEGY
Comprehension

TOPIC: American History—Battle of the Alamo
STUDENT ACTIVITY: Identifying the Facts

◆ RATIONALE

- Students will develop a concrete understanding of the key terms and concepts.

- Students will broaden their understanding of the Battle of the Alamo.

- Students will use their knowledge to answer higher-level thinking questions.

◆ OBJECTIVE

- Students will have a contextual understanding of the Battle of the Alamo.

◆ ENGAGEMENT

- Teacher can present a current event and lead a discussion using the worksheet structure to help students see the value of asking and answering questions to more fully understand an event.

◆ INSTRUCTIONAL SUPPORT

- Make and use a transparency of the worksheet to demonstrate to the class how to complete it.

- Allow students to work with partners to complete the worksheet.

- While some students are still working, ask students who have finished to answer the "To Think About" questions.

- Ask students to exchange worksheets and discuss their answers.

- After students have completed the worksheet, lead a discussion on the exercise.

- Encourage students to use the worksheet when studying for the test.

◆ ASSESSMENT SUPPORT

- During examinations, provide students with a blank or partially completed worksheet to assist them in organizing their thoughts before answering test questions, or allow students to use completed worksheets when answering open-ended and higher-level thinking questions.

- Allow students with documented writing deficits to orally answer open-ended and higher-level thinking questions.

ACTIVITY 4: Battle of the Alamo

Comprehension

STUDENT TIPS:
- Asking the questions *who, what, where, when,* and *why* helps you remember information.
- Use these questions when writing papers or answering questions in social studies.

DIRECTIONS:
Check your understanding of the Battle of the Alamo by answering the following questions using your textbook and other resources.

1. *Who* fought the Battle of the Alamo?

_____

_____

2. *What* happened at the Battle of the Alamo?

_____

_____

3. *Where* is the Alamo?

_____

_____

4. *When* was the Battle of the Alamo?

_____

_____

5. *Why* did the Battle of the Alamo take place?

_____

_____

◆ TO THINK ABOUT:
- Why was the Battle of the Alamo important?
- What might have changed the outcome of the battle?

TOPIC: American History—Nineteenth Century Reformers
STUDENT ACTIVITY: Creating a Poster

◆ RATIONALE

- Students will broaden their understanding about social reformers.

◆ OBJECTIVES

- Students will become familiar with a social reformer.

- Students will use research skills, critical thinking skills, and communication skills to create a poster that addresses the issue that the reformer was concerned about.

◆ ENGAGEMENT

- Teacher can begin class by talking about a well-known person. Lead students in a discussion about that person and what he or she has done by using the questions *who, what, where, when,* and *why.* Introduce the task.

◆ INSTRUCTIONAL SUPPORT

- Make suggestions to the class on various approaches to creating a poster using programs such as The Print Shop®, Microsoft Word®, AppleWorks®, or Adobe PageMaker®.

- Allow students to work with partners or small teams to complete the project.

- Supply students with sample interview questions.

- Require students with special needs to use an adapted format.

- Midway through the project, ask students to share their progress and offer suggestions to their classmates.

◆ ASSESSMENT SUPPORT

- During examinations, allow students to use their completed posters when answering open-ended and higher-level thinking questions.

ACTIVITY 5: Nineteenth Century Reformers

Finding and Organizing Details

STUDENT TIPS:
- Remember that to reform is to make a change in how something is done.
- Think about how posters are designed to capture the viewer's attention; try to use these ideas as you create your own.

DIRECTIONS:
Create a poster that tells about one of these famous people. Your poster should include information about and pictures of this person. To help you find information and pictures for your poster, use the Internet and resources at the library.

Your poster should answer these questions:

- *Who* is this person?
- *What* did he/she do?
- *Where* and *when* did he/she live?
- *Why* was this person's work important?

Social Reformers

—Ralph Waldo Emerson

—Thomas Gallaudet

—Lyman Beecher

—Dorothea Dix

—Henry David Thoreau

—Horace Mann

Participants in the Women's Movement

—Elizabeth Cady Stanton

—Susan B. Anthony

—Mary Lyon

—Amelia Jenks Bloomer

Abolitionists

—William Lloyd Garrison

—Sojourner Truth

—Frederick Douglass

—Harriet Tubman

◆ TO THINK ABOUT:
- Who are some important modern-day reformers?
- What can modern reformers learn from the techniques used by these historical figures?

ACTIVITY 6 TEACHING STRATEGY
Finding and Organizing Details

TOPIC: World History—Ancient Greek City-States
STUDENT ACTIVITY: Completing a Matrix

◆ RATIONALE

- Students will develop a concrete understanding of the key terms and concepts.

- Students will increase their knowledge of the ancient Greek city-states through research and questions.

- By identifying how concepts are similar and how they are different, students will have details about the topic to use when answering open-ended questions.

- Students will use their knowledge to answer higher-level thinking questions.

◆ OBJECTIVE

- Students will compare and contrast the city-states of Athens and Sparta.

◆ ENGAGEMENT

- Teacher can develop a sample matrix with the students to show them how it can help in organizing their information. A simple matrix might use two sports (baseball and hockey) and look at several factors such as: number of players, where played, when played, professional and amateur leagues, and opportunities for women. A third sport could also be added.

◆ INSTRUCTIONAL SUPPORT

- Allow students to work with partners.

- Complete parts of the matrix with the students to get them started.

- Reduce the number of categories for comparison to the few most important (government, economy, religion).

- Show students how to find data in the text and/or other materials (use of index and glossary, for example).

◆ ASSESSMENT SUPPORT

- Students can use the matrix as a study guide.

- Have students use the matrix to write an essay comparing and contrasting Athens and Sparta.

ACTIVITY 6: Ancient Greek City-States

Finding and Organizing Details

STUDENT TIPS:
- Look at those items that have already been filled in as an example to help you complete the chart.
- Use a few key words or phrases to complete the chart.

DIRECTIONS:
Use your textbook and other resources to complete this chart.

CITY-STATES	ATHENS	SPARTA
LOCATION		
GOVERNMENT	democracy—all free men who were citizens could vote	
ECONOMY		discouraged trade
RELIGION		
LITERATURE/ ART/CULTURE		
TECHNOLOGY		

◆ TO THINK ABOUT:
- Describe the most significant achievement of each of these city-states.
- How is the technology of today different from the technology of Athens and Sparta?

TOPIC: World History—Early World Religions
STUDENT ACTIVITY: Using a Four-Square Box

◆ RATIONALE

- Students develop an understanding of different religions and their importance in history.

◆ OBJECTIVE

- Students will review information on two world religions to understand their differences.

◆ ENGAGEMENT

- Teacher presents one or more of the following examples to show students how the Four-Square Box works. The key is that students understand how three facts are connected, whereas one is not, and why it is not connected.

A. Which one does not belong and why?

apple	pear
pizza	peach

Acceptable answers are "pizza" because it is not a fruit, or "apple," because it does not start with a "p."

B. Which one does not belong and why?

Greece	Italy
Los Angeles	France

An acceptable answer is "Los Angeles" because it is the only city and it is not in Europe.

◆ INSTRUCTIONAL SUPPORT

- Use this format to compare religions (such as Buddhism and Hinduism).

- Have students use the textbook to find information on religions.

- Students can work in pairs (with a "thinking partner").

- Students can make up their own boxes using other social studies facts that fall into the same category. Allow them to quiz each other.

◆ ASSESSMENT SUPPORT

- Students can make a chart showing the answer to the first "To Think About" question.

- The number of religions to be compared can be adapted to the learner's ability.

- Students can use the Internet or other resources to do a mini-research paper on one of the religions.

ACTIVITY 7: Early World Religions

Studying and Writing/Reviewing Main Ideas

STUDENT TIPS:
- The title of the box is a clue that helps you identify the correct facts.
- If you are having trouble deciding which fact does not belong, first decide which ones you know are correct. Then research the remaining ones in your textbook or other reference books.

DIRECTIONS:
Decide which of the facts does not belong in the boxes below and explain why it does not fit with the others.

BOX #1–CHRISTIANITY	
A. Followers of this religion believe that Jesus is the son of God.	**B.** The Romans persecuted early followers of this religion.
C. The Bible gives guidance on how to treat others and live a good life.	**D.** The prophet Muhammad received revelations from Allah.

In Box #1, fact _____ does not belong because _____

_____.

BOX #2–ISLAM	
A. The Koran is the Holy Scripture.	**B.** By A.D. 631, this had spread throughout the entire Arabian peninsula.
C. In A.D. 392, it became Rome's official religion.	**D.** A major belief is that law and religion cannot be separated.

In Box #2, fact _____ does not belong because _____

_____.

◆ **TO THINK ABOUT:**
- In which countries are these religions practiced today?
- Why do you think that people of different regions often practice different religions?

ACTIVITY 8 TEACHING STRATEGY
Critical Thinking

TOPIC: World History—The Byzantine Empire
STUDENT ACTIVITY: Making Inferences From Readings

◆ RATIONALE
- Students learn to draw conclusions based on pertinent facts.

◆ OBJECTIVE
- Students will make accurate inferences based on stated facts.

◆ ENGAGEMENT
- Teacher will write the following example on the board and ask the students what the best logical choice or inference is based on the facts. Teacher should use the following example to explain what an inference is.

  As Mr. Johnson drove down the icy road, he was thinking of the big basketball game. Suddenly, a deer ran out into the road in front of him.

  Ask the students what might happen next. Possible answers may include:
  - He slammed on the brakes and barely missed the deer.
  - He hit the deer and wrecked the car.
  - He turned off the road into a ditch.

- The key is that each of the inferences above is based on the facts and makes sense. A poor inference would be "We won the big game" because it is not the best logical conclusion based on the facts.

◆ INSTRUCTIONAL SUPPORT
- Provide an easy-to-understand passage from a newspaper or magazine to give students practice. A cartoon strip works well. Show the students the first two panels and ask them to infer (predict) what will happen next from multiple choices that you provide.

- Teach any new vocabulary.

- As students learn the skill, remove the multiple choices and have them write the inference and their reasons for choosing it.

◆ ASSESSMENT SUPPORT
- Allow students to use the activity sheet as a study guide before and/or during the test.

- Have students use the "To Think About" question as a topic for research.

- Ask students to make their own passages and inferences from the chapter, which they can exchange with their classmates.

ACTIVITY 8: The Byzantine Empire

Critical Thinking

STUDENT TIPS:
- Try to identify the main idea of a paragraph in one sentence.
- Think in general terms rather than specific terms when writing a conclusion.

DIRECTIONS:

Read the following passages. Then write the letter of the best inference, *or conclusion, based on your reading. Explain why you chose your answer.*

THE IMPORTANCE OF THE BYZANTINE EMPIRE

The Byzantine Empire lasted from A.D. 300–1453. It stretched across Eastern Europe and the Middle East. During the Middle Ages in Western Europe, much of what had been learned from the early Greeks and Romans was lost. The Byzantine Empire grew during this time. Laws and political practices were written down. These writings about the early times have taught us what life was like then.

A. The Middle Ages forced the Byzantine Empire to collapse.
B. If it were not for the Byzantine Empire, we would have lost much of what we learned from the Greeks and Romans.
C. The Byzantine Empire developed the modern Greek and Italian languages.

I chose answer _____ because _____

_____.

EMPEROR JUSTINIAN

Justinian become Emperor of the Byzantine Empire in A.D. 527. His wife, Theodora, was an effective advisor who helped improve the lives of women in the empire. Justinian's army stopped a revolt in Constantinople, the Byzantine capital, in A.D. 532. His armies also defeated later attacks from the Persians. This allowed him to expand the empire. Justinian chose a group to organize ancient Roman laws into the Justinian Code. Today in Europe, many laws are still based on this code.

A. Theodora helped conquer the Persians by organizing a women's army.
B. Justinian lived a long and happy life.
C. The Justinian Code has influenced today's laws in Europe.

I chose answer _____ because _____

_____.

◆ **TO THINK ABOUT:**
- Why is it important to have laws written down for people?

ACTIVITY 9 TEACHING STRATEGY
Organizing and Remembering

TOPIC: World History—Western Feudalism (A.D. 700–1100)
STUDENT ACTIVITY: Making Vocabulary Flash Cards

◆ RATIONALE
- By using three types of information about the key vocabulary, students will learn the concepts, not just the words.

◆ OBJECTIVE
- Students will make flash cards to help them remember key vocabulary terms.

◆ ENGAGEMENT
- Teacher can go over the following example to show students how to design their flash cards. Teacher can present the students with concrete ideas to help them remember key concepts.

◆ INSTRUCTIONAL SUPPORT
- Make some sample cards to practice with students.

- Allow students to work with partners to complete the flash cards.

- Pictures from magazines and other resources can be used for sketches.

- Have students quiz each other with flash cards.

- Encourage students to use flash cards when studying for tests.

◆ ASSESSMENT SUPPORT
- Students may be allowed to use cards to answer multiple-choice questions on tests.

- Students can use cards when studying for tests.

Key Word	Definition
DEMOCRACY	a government by the people

Sketch	Connections/Examples
BALLOT BOX	From a Greek word meaning "people"; the United States is a democracy; Cuba is not a democracy

ACTIVITY 9: Western Feudalism (A.D. 700–1100)

Organizing and Remembering

STUDENT TIPS:
- Check the Web for more information about feudalism:
  www.learner.org/exhibits/middleages/feudal.html
- It is helpful to make your vocabulary flash cards on thicker paper or poster board so that they will last longer.

DIRECTIONS:
- *In a dictionary or in the glossary of your textbook, find the definitions of these vocabulary terms:* vassal, serf, homage, chivalry, clergy, *and* fief.
- *Look at this example of a vocabulary flash card. Use it as a model to help you make the remaining cards for the above vocabulary words on separate pieces of paper.*

KEY WORD	DEFINITION
FEUDALISM	a type of government where a king or strong noble would give land to other nobles in exchange for protection

SKETCH	CONNECTIONS/EXAMPLES
	Western Europe; peasants worked on the land; castles were needed for protection during wars

◆ TO THINK ABOUT:
- At the present time, how is the United States protected in case of war?
- How does this protection differ from feudalism?

TOPIC: World History—The French Revolution
STUDENT ACTIVITY: Using a Venn Diagram

◆ RATIONALE

- By discussing ideas with a partner and completing a Venn diagram, students will learn about the topic from another point of view.

- Teacher will know problem areas for students and will be able to modify instruction for the class and/or individuals.

◆ OBJECTIVE

- Students will describe at least three causes of the French Revolution.

◆ ENGAGEMENT

- Teacher can begin the activity by leading a discussion on cause and effect using an example taken from a local sporting event such as *This past weekend our basketball team won. What were the causes or events that led to this victory?*

◆ INSTRUCTIONAL SUPPORT

- Make and use a transparency of the worksheet to demonstrate to the class how to complete it.

- Remind students to think about their answers before beginning the worksheet or talking to their partners.

- While some students are still working, ask students who have finished to answer the "To Think About" question.

- Ask sets of "thinking partners" to form "thinking quads" to discuss answers.

- After students have discussed the worksheet with groups, lead a class discussion.

◆ ASSESSMENT SUPPORT

- Allow students with documented writing deficits to orally answer open-ended and higher-level thinking questions.

ACTIVITY 10: The French Revolution

Checking for Understanding

STUDENT TIPS:
- Look at several different sources, including an encyclopedia, the Internet, and your text-book to find information about the causes of the French Revolution.
- Make sure you list all of the ideas that you and your partner agree upon.

DIRECTIONS:
List your ideas about what caused the French Revolution in Circle A. Then, list your partner's ideas about what caused the French Revolution in Circle B. Look for items that appear in both circles and write these items in Circle C.

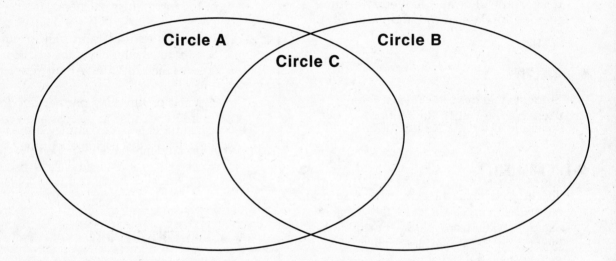

These are my ideas about the causes of the French Revolution.

These are the causes of the French Revolution that my partner and I agree on.

These are my partner's ideas about the causes of the French Revolution.

◆ TO THINK ABOUT:
- What long-term effects did the French Revolution have on the world?

ACTIVITY 11 TEACHING STRATEGY
Compare and Contrast

TOPIC: Civics—Preamble to the U.S. Constitution
STUDENT ACTIVITY: Ranking Importance

◆ RATIONALE

- By ranking the order of importance of the goals outlined in the Preamble to the Constitution, students will have details about the topic to use when answering open-ended questions.

- Students will use their knowledge to answer higher-level thinking questions.

◆ OBJECTIVE

- Students will analyze and evaluate the goals of government stated in the Preamble to the U.S. Constitution.

◆ ENGAGEMENT

- Teacher describes the following situation:

  Rebecca is about to board a train for a six-hour ride. She has enough money to buy either a paperback book that she has been looking forward to reading or a sandwich. Which item should she purchase?

- Teacher asks students to work with a partner to decide what Rebecca should do and why. Teacher calls on groups to discuss possible answers. Teacher should introduce the vocabulary underlined on the student worksheet.

◆ INSTRUCTIONAL SUPPORT

- Allow students to work with partners to complete the worksheet.

- Review and explain new and unfamiliar vocabulary from the Preamble.

- Remind students to think about their answers before beginning the worksheet or before talking to their partners.

- While some students are still working, ask students who have finished to answer the "To Think About" question.

- After students have completed the worksheet, lead a discussion about the activity.

- Encourage students to use this worksheet as a study guide.

◆ ASSESSMENT SUPPORT

- During examinations, allow students to use the completed worksheet when answering open-ended and higher-level thinking questions.

- Allow students with documented writing deficits to orally answer open-ended and higher-level thinking questions.

ACTIVITY 11: Preamble to the U.S. Constitution

Compare and Contrast

STUDENT TIPS:
- Ranking items requires you to know what each item means and to think about the items from different points of view.
- Before ranking the constitutional goals, write a phrase that describes how each goal affects you, your family, and your friends.

DIRECTIONS:
- *Read the Preamble to the Constitution of the United States. Review the underlined vocabulary before you begin.*
- *The Preamble to the Constitution states the six reasons our government was established. All of these goals are important, but is one more important than another? List the following goals in order of importance to you. Explain why the goal is important.*

 We, the people of the United States, in Order to form a more perfect Union, establish Justice, insure domestic Tranquility (<u>Tranquillity</u>), provide for the common defence (<u>defense</u>), promote the <u>general Welfare</u>, and secure the Blessings of <u>Liberty</u> to ourselves and our <u>Posterity</u>, do <u>ordain</u> and establish this Constitution for the United States of America.

REASONS WHY OUR GOVERNMENT WAS ESTABLISHED	CONSTITUTIONAL GOALS THAT ARE IMPORTANT TO ME AND WHY
A. To form a more perfect Union	1.
B. Establish justice	2.
C. Insure domestic tranquility	3.
D. Provide for the common defense	4.
E. Promote the general welfare	5.
F. Secure the blessings of liberty to ourselves and our posterity	6.

◆ TO THINK ABOUT:
- Would you have included other reasons in the Preamble for forming our government?

ACTIVITY 12 TEACHING STRATEGY
Checking for Understanding

TOPIC: Civics—The Bill of Rights

STUDENT ACTIVITY: Writing a One-Minute Paper

◆ RATIONALE

- By identifying what students have learned about a particular topic, they will recognize misconceptions they may have had about it.

- Teacher will know students' problem areas and will be able to modify instruction for the class and/or individuals.

◆ OBJECTIVE

- Students will identify some of the most important aspects of the First Amendment from the Bill of Rights.

◆ ENGAGEMENT

- Teacher can begin the activity by conducting a "One-Minute Survey." Teacher poses the following questions and asks students to respond by raising their hands. It is helpful for some students to explain why they chose a particular answer.

  1. *Raise your hand if you think that studying the Bill of Rights is important to a middle school student.*
  2. *Raise your hand if you think that studying the Bill of Rights is important to an adult.*

- The students' responses should help teacher and students assess their understanding of the application of the Bill of Rights in everyday life.

◆ INSTRUCTIONAL SUPPORT

- Make and use a transparency of the worksheet to demonstrate to the class how to complete it.

- Review and explain new and unfamiliar vocabulary contained in the First Amendment.

- Remind students to think about their answers before beginning the worksheet or before talking to their partners.

- Ask sets of "thinking partners" to form "thinking quads" to discuss answers.

- Lead a discussion about patterns of understanding and misunderstanding as identified by the students on the worksheet.

◆ ASSESSMENT SUPPORT

- Allow students with documented writing deficits to orally answer open-ended and higher-level thinking questions.

ACTIVITY 12: The Bill of Rights

Checking for Understanding

STUDENT TIPS:
- Underline each freedom listed in the First Amendment of the Bill of Rights to help organize your thoughts.
- Think about which freedoms are important to you as an adolescent, then respond to the first question.

DIRECTIONS:
Read the First Amendment from the Bill of Rights and answer the questions below.

★★★★★★★★★★★★★★★★★★★

Congress shall make no law respecting an establishment of religion, or prohibiting the free exercise thereof; or abridging the freedom of speech, or of the press; or the right of the people peaceably to assemble, and to petition the Government for a redress of grievances.

1. What is the *most important* thing you learned about the First Amendment?

_____

_____

2. Name one way the First Amendment affected your life today.

_____

_____

3. Why is this amendment important to you?

_____

_____

◆ TO THINK ABOUT:
- What questions do you still want answered about the First Amendment?
- How does the First Amendment affect your life? Your family? Your school? The city/town where you live?

ACTIVITY 13 TEACHING STRATEGY
Checking for Understanding

TOPIC: Civics—The Amendments to the U.S. Constitution
STUDENT ACTIVITY: Completing a KWL Chart

◆ RATIONALE

- By starting a KWL chart (What I Know, What I Want to Know, What I Have Learned), students will recognize their knowledge and misunderstandings about a particular topic.

- By using a matrix the students will become aware of what they know about the Amendments to the Constitution.

◆ OBJECTIVE

- Students will identify facts about the amendments.

◆ ENGAGEMENT

- Teacher can begin the activity by conducting a "One-Minute Survey." Students should understand that answering the survey helps clarify the thinking process. Teacher poses the following questions and asks students to respond by raising their hands. It is helpful for some students to explain why they chose a particular answer.

  1. *Raise your hand if you think that Columbus landed on the shore of the United States.*
  2. *Raise your hand if you think that only the United States of America has a Constitution.*
  3. *Raise your hand if you think that countries must be old to have a fair government.*

- Teacher can lead a discussion about the effects of learning on our opinions and explain how when we learn new facts our opinions often change.

◆ INSTRUCTIONAL SUPPORT

- Make and use a transparency of the worksheet to demonstrate to the class how to complete it using information on what they did and did not know about the Amendments.

- Remind students to think about their answers before beginning the worksheet or before talking to their partners.

- While some students are still working, ask students who have finished to answer the "To Think About" question.

- Ask students to exchange worksheets and discuss their answers.

- After students have completed the worksheet, lead a discussion about the exercise.

◆ ASSESSMENT SUPPORT

- During examinations, allow students to use the completed worksheet when answering open-ended and higher-level thinking questions.

ACTIVITY 13: The Amendments to the U.S. Constitution

Checking for Understanding

STUDENT TIPS:
- A KWL chart helps you identify **what you know**, **what you want to know**, and **what you have learned**.
- Read editorials in your local newspaper to see how the amendments affect people's everyday lives.

DIRECTIONS:
Fill in the chart based on what you know and information from your textbook.

AMENDMENT	WHAT I KNOW	WHAT I WANT TO KNOW	WHAT I LEARNED	HOW THIS AMENDMENT AFFECTS ME
SIXTEENTH				
NINETEENTH				
TWENTY-SECOND				
TWENTY-SIXTH				

◆ TO THINK ABOUT:
- Write an amendment that you think should be added to the Constitution in the twenty-first century.

TOPIC: Civics—How a Federal Bill Becomes a Law

STUDENT ACTIVITY: Sequencing Events

◆ RATIONALE

- Students will develop a concrete, contextual understanding of the key terms and the process by which a federal bill becomes a law.

- Students will broaden their understanding by asking questions and doing research about the making of a law.

- Students will use their knowledge to answer higher-level thinking questions.

◆ OBJECTIVE

- Students will construct an understanding about how a federal bill becomes a law.

◆ ENGAGEMENT

- On a transparency teacher guides students in a discussion of how they obtain a high school diploma. Ask students to sequence the learning process from first grade until they graduate from high school. Emphasize that there are certain procedures and tests that must be completed during this process. Apply this sequencing to the stages for how a bill becomes a law.

◆ INSTRUCTIONAL SUPPORT

- Make and use a transparency of the worksheet to demonstrate to the class how to complete it.

- Allow students to work with partners to complete the worksheet.

- Partially complete the worksheet for some students.

- Remind students to think about their answers before beginning the worksheet or before talking to their partners.

- While some students are still working, ask students who have finished to answer the "To Think About" question.

- After students have completed the worksheet, lead a discussion about the exercise.

- Encourage students to use the worksheet when studying for tests.

◆ ASSESSMENT SUPPORT

- During examinations, provide students with a blank or partially completed worksheet to assist them in organizing their thoughts before answering test questions, or allow students to use completed worksheets when answering open-ended and higher-level thinking questions.

- Allow students with documented writing deficits to orally answer open-ended and higher-level thinking questions.

ACTIVITY 15: How a Federal Bill Becomes a Law

Thinking About Data

STUDENT TIPS:
- Identify your state's representatives. Look in the local newspaper to see how they voted on certain issues.
- Follow a national bill through newspapers, the Internet, or television until it is tabled or is signed or vetoed by the president. Seeing the practical application will help you better understand the necessary steps.

DIRECTIONS:
Complete the chart to show the sequence of how a federal bill becomes a law.

INTRODUCTION OF BILL	
HOUSE	
SENATE	

COMMITTEE ACTION	
HOUSE	
SENATE	

ACTION BY CONGRESS	
HOUSE	
SENATE	

ENACTMENT INTO LAW	
PRESIDENT	

◆ **TO THINK ABOUT:**
- Can the president make a law without approval by Congress?

ACTIVITY 16 TEACHING STRATEGY
Acquiring Geographic Information

TOPIC: Geography—Globe Skills/Hemispheres
STUDENT ACTIVITY: Identifying Places on a Globe

◆ RATIONALE

- Using key vocabulary, students will be able to locate places on a globe.

- Students will become familiar with the globe and will be able to identify in which parts of the world different countries are located.

◆ OBJECTIVE

- Students will determine in which hemisphere different places are located.

◆ ENGAGEMENT

- Teacher can cut an orange into parts to show the hemispheres on the globe. Placing string around a globe to show the Prime Meridian and the Equator can also be helpful.

- Teacher can cut paper to fit around the globe, moving it to show the different hemispheres.

◆ INSTRUCTIONAL SUPPORT

- Explain to students that imaginary lines are used to help find places on maps and globes.

- Show students why a globe is a more accurate representation of the earth than a flat map.

- Encourage students to work in pairs to locate places on the globe.

- Review the key vocabulary.

◆ ASSESSMENT SUPPORT

- Help students locate countries on a globe (or map) and identify in which hemispheres they are located.

- Ask students to name places that are in certain hemispheres.

ACTIVITY 16: Globe Skills/Hemispheres

Acquiring Geographic Information

STUDENT TIPS:
- Remember that the lines of longitude and latitude are imaginary lines.
- If you do not remember what a hemisphere is, look up the term in a dictionary or your textbook's glossary.

Review these facts below about hemispheres.
- Imaginary lines are drawn on the globe (and on most maps) to help us locate places.
- Imaginary lines from north to south are called *lines of longitude*.
- Imaginary lines from east to west are called *lines of latitude*.
- The *Prime Meridian* is 0° longitude and splits the earth into Western and Eastern Hemispheres.
- The *Equator* is 0° latitude and splits the earth into Northern and Southern Hemispheres.
- All places on the earth are in at least two *hemispheres*.

DIRECTIONS:
Write the hemispheres for each place listed below. Some places may be found in more than two hemispheres. The United States is completed as an example.

PLACE	HEMISPHERES
United States	Western, Northern
Japan	
Australia	
Arctic Ocean	
Turkey	
Argentina	
Antarctica	
Canada	
South Africa	
China	
New Zealand	

◆ TO THINK ABOUT:
- Why do geographers use imaginary lines to locate places on the earth?

ACTIVITY 17 TEACHING STRATEGY
Checking for Understanding

TOPIC: Geography—Plate Tectonics
STUDENT ACTIVITY: Writing a One-Minute Paper

◆ RATIONALE

- By identifying what students have learned about a particular topic, they will recognize misconceptions they may have had about it.

- The teacher will know areas of student misunderstanding and will be able to modify instruction for the class and/or individuals.

◆ OBJECTIVE

- Students will identify why the study of plate tectonics is important.

◆ ENGAGEMENT

- Teacher can begin the activity by conducting a "One-Minute Survey." Students should understand that answering the survey helps clarify the thinking process. Teacher poses the following questions and asks students to respond by raising their hands.

  1. *Raise your hand if you think that studying about earthquakes is important.*
  2. *Raise your hand if you think that studying landforms is important.*
  3. *Raise your hand if you think that studying about tidal waves is important.*

- Allow students the opportunity to give the reasons for their answers.

- Teacher reminds students that the movement of the earth's plates causes these events. Refer them to sections in their textbooks where this topic is discussed.

◆ INSTRUCTIONAL SUPPORT

- Remind students to think about their answers before beginning the worksheet or talking to their partners.

- While some students are still working on the worksheet, ask students who have finished to begin working on the "To Think About" questions.

- After everyone has completed the worksheet, ask students to exchange worksheets and discuss their answers with their partners.

- Lead a discussion with students about their answers.

◆ ASSESSMENT SUPPORT

- Allow students with documented writing deficits to orally answer open-ended and higher-level thinking questions.

- Encourage students to find out the answers to their "To Think About" questions as a homework and/or type of assessment.

ACTIVITY 17: Plate Tectonics

Checking for Understanding

STUDENT TIPS:
- Review your class notes on plate tectonics and make a list of all of the facts that you know.
- Rank the facts from least important to most important to help you organize your thoughts.

DIRECTIONS:
Answer the following questions based on what you have learned.

1. Why do scientists study plate tectonics?

_____

_____

_____

_____

2. What is the *most important* thing you learned about plate tectonics?

_____

_____

_____

_____

3. Why is this important to you?

_____

_____

_____

_____

◆ **TO THINK ABOUT:**
- What are some instruments that measure the activities of plate tectonics?
- How does the study of plate tectonics affect the architecture of buildings?

TOPIC: Geography—Bodies of Water

STUDENT ACTIVITY: Completing a Chart

◆ **RATIONALE**

- Students will gain an understanding of the geographical traits of different regions.

- Students will develop skills necessary to read and understand maps.

◆ **OBJECTIVE**

- Students will use map vocabulary as they organize bodies of water in a chart.

◆ **ENGAGEMENT**

- Teacher asks students *What percentage (how much) of the world's water is suitable for drinking?*

- Teacher shares the following data and points to the bodies of water on a map:

  - *Ninety-seven percent of the world's water is saltwater, which we can't drink.*
  - *Two percent of the world's freshwater is frozen in ice sheets and glaciers.*
  - *Only 1% of the world's water is suitable for drinking.*

- A world map that clearly shows bodies of water is best for this student activity. Other maps may be used, but will require the teacher to make some modifications to the student activity.

◆ **INSTRUCTIONAL SUPPORT**

- If necessary, reduce the number of bodies of water the student needs to find (from five to three rivers, for example).

- Help students find a few of the bodies of water to get them started on this activity.

- Students can complete this activity in pairs (with a "thinking partner").

- Guide the students through answering the "To Think About" question.

◆ **ASSESSMENT SUPPORT**

- Point to different bodies of water on a map and have students identify what types they are.

- Assign students a mini-research paper on topics such as: desalinization; groundwater problems in areas such as Massachusetts or Florida; the Ice Age; or the use of icebergs and glaciers for drinking water.

ACTIVITY 18: Bodies of Water

Reading a Map

STUDENT TIPS:
- If you do not remember what a strait, bay, or gulf is, look in a dictionary or the glossary of your geography book.
- Look at a topography map to locate rivers, lakes, oceans, and gulfs.

DIRECTIONS:
Use a world map to complete the chart.

BODIES OF WATER		
FIVE RIVERS	**TWO OCEANS**	
1.	1.	
2.	2.	
3.		
4.	**TWO SEAS**	
5.	1.	
	2.	
FIVE LAKES		
1.	**TWO GULFS**	
2.	1.	
3.	2.	
4.		
5.	**TWO BAYS**	
	1.	
TWO COUNTRIES WHERE GLACIERS ARE FOUND	2.	
1.	**TWO STRAITS**	
2.	1.	
	2.	

◆ **TO THINK ABOUT:**
- Why would it be important for a country to be located near rivers or oceans?

ACTIVITY 19 TEACHING STRATEGY
Comprehension and Memory

TOPIC: Geography—The Andean Countries
STUDENT ACTIVITY: Using Memory Clues

◆ RATIONALE

- Students will develop a concrete understanding of the key terms and concepts.

- Students will broaden their understanding of the geography of the Andean countries.

- Students will use their knowledge to answer higher-level thinking questions.

◆ OBJECTIVE

- Students will review and remember key terms about the Andean countries.

◆ ENGAGEMENT

- Teacher can discuss ways of remembering unconnected bits of information and give examples. The use of the acronym "HOMES" to remember the names of the Great Lakes is a good example. [H = Huron; O = Ontario; M = Michigan; E = Erie; S = Superior]

◆ INSTRUCTIONAL SUPPORT

- Allow students to work with partners to complete the worksheet.

- Ask students to exchange worksheets and discuss their answers.

- Ask students to quiz each other with worksheets.

- While some students are still working, ask students who have finished to answer the "To Think About" question.

- After all students have completed the worksheet, lead a discussion about their answers.

- Encourage students to use the worksheet as a study guide when preparing for tests.

◆ ASSESSMENT SUPPORT

- During examinations, provide students with a blank or partially completed worksheet to assist them in organizing their thoughts before answering test questions, or allow students to use completed worksheets when answering open-ended and higher-level thinking questions.

- Allow students with documented writing deficits to orally answer open-ended and higher-level thinking questions.

ACTIVITY 19: The Andean Countries

Comprehension and Memory

STUDENT TIPS:
- An *acronym* is a word formed from the beginning letter (or letters) of other words.
- Use acronyms to help you when memorizing a series of facts.

DIRECTIONS:
Check your understanding of the Andean countries by answering the following questions. A memory clue is given for each question.

1. Name the six Andean countries.

> *Memory clue*—Use the acronym PECBAC, which represents the first letter of each country.

_____

_____

_____

2. Which country was the center of the Inca Empire?

> *Memory clue*—Note that the answer has the same number of letters as Inca.

_____

_____

_____

3. Name the four major landforms of Argentina.

> *Memory clue*—Remember PPAL as an acronym.

_____

_____

_____

◆ TO THINK ABOUT:
- Describe what a car trip from La Paz, Bolivia, south to Cape Horn would be like based on what you know. Make sure you describe the changes in climate and elevation that you would expect to experience. Name the countries that you would travel through.

ACTIVITY 20 TEACHING STRATEGY
Compare and Contrast

TOPIC: Geography—Israel and Jordan
STUDENT ACTIVITY: Using a Venn Diagram

◆ RATIONALE

- By identifying how concepts are similar and how they are different, students will have details about the topic to use when answering open-ended questions.

- Students will use their knowledge to answer higher-level thinking questions.

◆ OBJECTIVE

- Students will organize information to compare and contrast Israel and Jordan.

◆ ENGAGEMENT

- Teacher can show two posters and ask students to compare them using the following questions:

  1. *How are they alike?* (Write a list of suggested similarities on the board.)
  2. *How are they different regarding color, size, image, and purpose?* (Write a list of suggested differences by category on the board.)

- Teacher discusses answers and introduces the Venn diagram worksheet.

◆ INSTRUCTIONAL SUPPORT

- Make and use a transparency of the worksheet to demonstrate to the class how to complete it.

- Allow students to work with partners to complete the worksheet.

- Partially complete the worksheet with some students.

- Remind students to think about their answers before beginning the worksheet or before talking to their partners.

- While some students are still working, ask students who have finished to answer the "To Think About" question.

- After students have completed the worksheet, lead a discussion about the exercise.

- Encourage students to use this worksheet as a study guide.

◆ ASSESSMENT SUPPORT

- During examinations, provide students with a blank or partially completed worksheet to assist them in organizing their thoughts before answering test questions, or allow students to use the completed worksheet when answering open-ended and higher-level thinking questions.

- Allow students with documented writing deficits to orally answer open-ended and higher-level thinking questions.

ACTIVITY 20: Israel and Jordan

Compare and Contrast

STUDENT TIPS:
- A Venn diagram, like the one in this exercise, helps you to visually understand how topics are alike and different.
- You can develop a Venn diagram when you write comparing and contrasting essays.

DIRECTIONS:
List facts that are true about Israel in Circle A. Then, list facts that are true about Jordan in Circle B. Look for facts that are true for both countries and write them in Circle C.

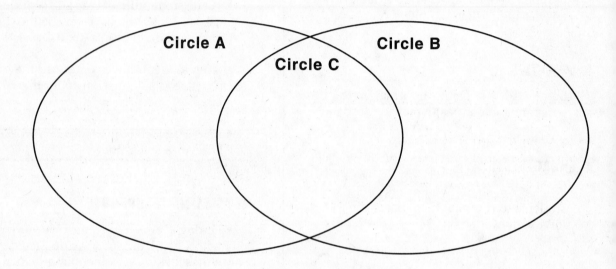

| These facts are true about Israel. | These facts are true for both Israel and Jordan. | These facts are true about Jordan. |

◆ TO THINK ABOUT:
- How might these neighboring countries improve their relations with each other?

Answer Key

Chapter I—American History

Student Activity 1: Major European Explorers

MAJOR EUROPEAN EXPLORERS			
COUNTRY	EXPLORER	DATES	ACHIEVEMENTS
ENGLAND	Cabot Hudson	1497–1501 1610–1611	rediscovered Newfoundland explored Hudson Bay
FRANCE	Verrazano Cartier Champlain Marquette/Joliet La Salle	1524 1534–1542 1603–1615 1673 1666–1682	explored New York harbor explored St. Lawrence River explored St. Lawrence River and founded Quebec explored Mississippi River explored Great Lakes; founded Louisiana
PORTUGAL	Dias Da Gama Cabral	1487–1488 1497–1499 1500	sailed around tip of Africa sailed around Africa to India sailed to Brazil
SPAIN	Columbus Ponce de Leon Magellan Da Vaca Coronado De Soto Cabrillo	1492–1504 1508–1513 1519–1522 1530 1540–1542 1539–1543 1542–1543	explored islands of the Caribbean Sea explored Puerto Rico and Florida first to sail around the world explored northern Mexico and Brazil explored southwestern North America explored Mississippi River explored west coast of North America

Student Activity 2: History of Massachusetts

Student newspaper articles and interviews will vary, but should contain accurate information indicating research about the historical event chosen by the student. Completed student activities should include the banner, headline, feature story, and interview with historical character.

Student Activity 3: New England Colonies

NEW ENGLAND COLONIES			
COLONY	FOUNDER	DATE FOUNDED	REASON WHY IT WAS FOUNDED
MASSACHUSETTS • Massachusetts Bay Colony • Plymouth	 Winthrop Bradford	 1630 1620	 religious freedom religious freedom
NEW HAMPSHIRE	Gorges, Mason, Wheelwright	1622	trade and fishing
RHODE ISLAND	Williams	1636	religious freedom
CONNECTICUT	Hooker	1636	fur trade, farming, religious freedom, and political freedom

Student Activity 4: Battle of the Alamo

1. *Who* fought the Battle of the Alamo? United States and Mexico

2. *What* happened at the Battle of the Alamo? After 12 days Santa Anna and the Mexican army defeated the Texans; however, the Texans gained valuable time to organize a new government.

3. *Where* is the Alamo? San Antonio, Texas

4. *When* was the Battle of the Alamo? February 23–March 6, 1836

5. *Why* did the Battle of the Alamo take place? In December 1835, Texans liberated San Antonio from a Mexican army. On March 2, 1836, the American settlers and Tejanos declared the independence of the Republic of Texas.

Student Activity 5: Nineteenth Century Reformers

Student posters will vary, but should contain accurate information indicating research about the person chosen by the student.

Chapter II—World History

Student Activity 6: Ancient Greek City-States

CITY-STATES	ATHENS	SPARTA
LOCATION	northeast of Peloponnesus on a peninsula of central Greece named Attica	Peloponnesus, a peninsula in southern Greece
GOVERNMENT	democracy; all free men who were citizens could vote	democracy; kings led military; male assembly; military society
ECONOMY	promoted trade	discouraged trade
RELIGION	worshipped gods—Athena brought special protection	worshipped gods
LITERATURE/ART/CULTURE	built the Parthenon; bronze and clay statues and vases; playwright Aeschylus wrote "The Oresteia"	emphasis on military, artisans from conquered territories worked for the Spartans
TECHNOLOGY	important discoveries in science	lagged behind other city-states in intellectual accomplishments

Student Activity 7: Early World Religions

Box #1–D; it describes Islam, not Christianity
Box #2–C; it describes Christianity, not Islam

Student Activity 8: The Byzantine Empire

Passage #1–B, because it is the only answer directly based on facts in the passage
Passage #2–C, because the other two answers were not directly stated in the passage

Student Activity 9: Western Feudalism (A.D. 700-1100)

Student flash cards will vary, but should follow the model shown. Each flash card should contain a definition, a sketch that relates to the word, and a sentence or phrase that provides a connection with the word.

Student Activity 10: The French Revolution

Student answers will vary but may include: absolute power of the monarchy; desire of the people for a better life; the unfair French class system; and government financial crises (debts, taxes, food shortages).

Chapter III—Civics

Student Activity 11: Preamble to the U.S. Constitution

Student answers will vary based on how they rank their reasons.

Student Activity 12: The Bill of Rights

Student answers will vary, but should reflect an understanding of the importance of the Bill of Rights in everyday life. Students should articulate why the First Amendment is important in their lives and apply this to a more general perception of how it is important for all of society.

Student Activity 13: The Amendments to the U.S. Constitution

KWL charts will vary from student to student based on their knowledge and what they still want to learn. This technique can be applied to any information that students are asked to analyze.

Student Activity 14: Rights and Responsibilities

Student flash cards will vary, but should follow the model shown. Each flash card should contain a definition, a sketch that relates to the word, and a sentence or phrase that provides a connection with the word.

Student Activity 15: How a Federal Bill Becomes a Law

INTRODUCTION OF BILL	
HOUSE	A member introduces a bill and it is sent to a committee for study. The same bill is introduced in the Senate.
SENATE	A member introduces a bill and it is sent to a committee for study. The same bill is introduced in the House.

COMMITTEE ACTION	
HOUSE	The committee holds hearings, makes changes, and recommends passage.
SENATE	The committee holds hearings, makes changes, and recommends passage.

ACTION BY CONGRESS	
HOUSE	The House debates and passes its form of the bill.
SENATE	The Senate debates and passes its form of the bill.
The House and Senate members confer and reach a compromise on a single form of the bill. House and Senate approve the compromise and send it to the president.	

ENACTMENT INTO LAW	
PRESIDENT	The president signs the bill into law or vetoes the bill. Congress may override the president's veto by a 2/3 majority vote.

Chapter IV—Geography

Student Activity 16: Globe Skills/Hemispheres

PLACE	HEMISPHERE
United States	Western, Northern
Japan	Eastern, Northern
Australia	Eastern, Southern
Arctic Ocean	Eastern, Western, Northern
Turkey	Eastern, Northern
Argentina	Western, Southern
Antarctica	Eastern, Western, Southern
Canada	Western, Northern
South Africa	Eastern, Southern
China	Eastern, Northern
New Zealand	Eastern, Southern

Student Activity 17: Plate Tectonics

Student answers will vary, but should indicate a comprehension of the importance of the study of plate tectonics.

Student Activity 18: Bodies of Water

BODIES OF WATER			
FIVE RIVERS		**TWO OCEANS**	
1. Nile		1. Indian Ocean	
2. Amazon		2. Arctic Ocean	
3. Xi			
4. Po		**TWO SEAS**	
5. Ural		1. Baltic Sea	
		2. Bering Sea	
FIVE LAKES			
1. Michigan		**TWO GULFS**	
2. Montana		1. Persian Gulf	
3. Albert		2. Gulf of Mexico	
4. Winnipeg			
5. Nicaragua		**TWO BAYS**	
		1. Bay of Biscay	
TWO COUNTRIES WHERE GLACIERS ARE FOUND		2. Bay of Bengal	
1. Switzerland		**TWO STRAITS**	
2. United States		1. Bering Strait	
		2. Strait of Magellan	

Student Activity 19: The Andean Countries

1. Peru, Ecuador, Colombia, Bolivia, Argentina, Chile (PECBAC)
2. Peru
3. Pampas, Patagonia, Andes, Lowlands (PPAL)

Student Activity 20: Israel and Jordan

Answers will vary for Circles A and B but may include facts about religion, economy, and government. Circle C could include climate, culture, and location among other facts that are shared.